MW0102585A

# Fulfilling My Father's Dream
## *Siv Ashley's Life in America*

## Siv Ashley

# Fulfilling My Father's Dream
## Siv Ashley's Life in America

Siv Ashley

Paws and Claws Publishing, LLC
High Point, NC

Text and photographs copyright 2018 by Siv Ashley. All rights reserved. No part of this book may be reproduced or transmitted in any form or by any means, electronic or mechanical, including photography, recording, or any information storage and retrieval system, without permission in writing from the publisher. The only exceptions are brief excerpts and reviews.

**Book and Cover Designer:** Jennifer Tipton Cappoen
**Editor:** Lynn Bemer Coble

PCBooks is an imprint of Paws and Claws Publishing, LLC.
1589 Skeet Club Road, Suite 102-175
High Point, NC 27265
www.PawsandClawsPublishing.com
info@pawsandclawspublishing.com


ISBN #978-1-946198-11-2
Printed in the United States

# Dedication

I would like to dedicate this book to Jefferson United Methodist Church for giving me the opportunity to come to America and pursue my dreams and my father's dream before mine.

I would also like to dedicate this book to the faculty, staff, and students of Jefferson Elementary School and Ashe Central High School who helped me learn and adapt to life in America.

I would ultimately like to thank God for allowing me to live and grow through Him. His provided strength holds me together and I am forever grateful.

## In Memory of Jennie Hightower

*Jennie Hightower was a member of Jefferson United Methodist Church. My family arrived from Thailand at the airport in Charlotte, North Carolina, in 1979, and Jennie was there with Reverend Worth Sweet (Pappy Sweet) to deliver us to our new home. She was very supportive of us and helpful in many ways. She loved the Lord, and she loved us. Jennie and several others in the church nurtured us from the time we arrived. Jennie was just like her mother who was on the Mission Board of Jefferson United Methodist Church.*

*I was glad that I was able to visit with Jennie three weeks before she died on May 23, 2016. She has been and will be greatly missed by her family, her friends, and my family.*

# Contents

Excerpt from Chapter Six and Prologue . . . . . . . . . . . . . . . . . 9

Chapter 1: Coming to America . . . . . . . . . . . . . . . . . . . . . . . 13

Chapter 2: The Life I Didn't Expect . . . . . . . . . . . . . . . . . . . 19

Chapter 3: Memories of School . . . . . . . . . . . . . . . . . . . . . . 25

Chapter 4: Things Begin to Decline . . . . . . . . . . . . . . . . . . . 35

Chapter 5: Flashback to a Better Time . . . . . . . . . . . . . . . . . 43

Chapter 6: My Living Nightmare . . . . . . . . . . . . . . . . . . . . . 57

Chapter 7: I Abandon God . . . . . . . . . . . . . . . . . . . . . . . . . 61

Chapter 8: Tia and Ty As Young Adults . . . . . . . . . . . . . . . . . 65

Chapter 9: Haiti Mission Trip . . . . . . . . . . . . . . . . . . . . . . . 69

Chapter 10: Ongoing Speeches and Special Thanks . . . . . . . . 75

## Excerpt from Chapter Six and Prologue

S uddenly things around me weren't clearly outlined, and I was having trouble figuring out exactly what was happening. I abruptly realized that I had abandoned my disabled brother Maine at the children's work camp in Cambodia! I knew that he was severely injured. I had only random memories of the woman at the pit telling me I had to leave and never turn back. Those fleeting memories quickly came and left. Panicked and sickened at the thought of leaving my own little brother to die, I rushed back to the pit where I had left him. But before I could reach him, there were Red soldiers pulling him away from me. The closer I got to Maine, the farther away the soldiers pulled him from my reach. I was running toward him as fast as I could, screaming for them to let him go. But I couldn't see their faces clearly, and I couldn't even tell if it were actually Maine whom they were so intently dragging away from me. My panic increased as the figures became more blurred. I felt such overwhelming agony and heartbreak as the realization hit that Maine was fading away from me, and I could never reach him. Suddenly I saw a bright light in front of me, and I woke up with sweat running down my face.

I realized that I was standing in the middle of the street. Kenny and others were calling out to me. I was having…night terrors that involved sleepwalking and nightmares….I had kept details about my past a secret from Kenny. I didn't talk much about all of the horror and trauma that I experienced in the Cambodian work camp....I had night terrors from the time I left Cambodia until well into my marriage....I was reliving what I went through in the work camps and leaving my brother who had died before I escaped.

...I assume that the woman at the pit was truthful and [Maine] is dead, but there will always be a part of me that will hold on to that memory. All that I experienced in the Cambodian work camp was a living nightmare. Ever since leaving Cambodia in 1979, I had been living with post-traumatic stress disorder (PTSD)....

*I had to get past leaving my brother behind....*

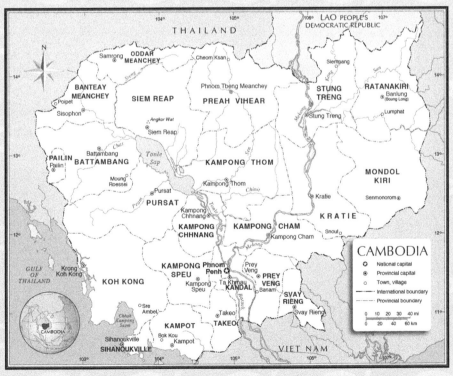

"But the Lord was with Joseph, and showed him mercy, and gave him favor in the sight of the keeper of the prison."
Genesis 39:21
(KJV)

## Chapter 1

# Coming to America

From April 1975 to May 1979, I lived in a children's work camp run by the Khmer Rouge in Cambodia. My life there was a living hell. All of my immediate family members died in the work camps during those years: my grandmother, my sisters, my mother, my father, and my brothers. Finally I escaped from the work camp with a group of Cambodians. An American soldier came out of the jungle and rescued me from a mountaintop. Then he carried me and later walked with me to the safe camp in Thailand. I arrived at the refugee camp in Thailand as Lum Siv Lang in May of 1979. In July, my remaining family and I were sponsored by Jefferson United Methodist Church in Ashe County, North Carolina, to come live in the United States. It was the hope we had been looking for and the opportunity of a lifetime.

I was in awe at the airport in Thailand. We had never seen a plane before. The only thing we had ever ridden was an elephant! We didn't understand the concept of flight. We knew that birds flew and that some monkeys could swing between trees, but the idea of an airplane excited us. I was very nervous as we boarded.

At that point, my biological aunt, Ly Puoy Houng, and my

uncle, Nguon Chou Sov, had stepped in to substitute for my parents who died in the work camps. I would eventually grow to call them Mom and Dad. My two younger cousins were then my little sisters. We only had one small bag for all five of us. We didn't have a translator on the plane, which made communication difficult. We had to make connections with another flight in Los Angeles before we would arrive at our final destination of Charlotte, North Carolina. But God was on our side and people directed us where to go and what to do.

After finding our seats on the plane, the flight stewards brought us food and drinks, though I was in such awe that I have no idea what they gave us. We saw other people on the plane eating from trays of food, so we followed their lead and ate ours. We weren't aware that there was a bathroom on the plane, so we went the entire time in the air without using the bathroom. It took around 15 hours to fly from the Thailand airport to the Los Angeles airport.

When we arrived in the United States, my family and I were in complete shock and didn't know what to do. We were just as clueless as we were when we started our trip and were even more overwhelmed. We stood there at the end of the terminal with our mouths gaping open in disbelief. This was a massively different airport from the one in which we boarded, bustling with people and an abundance of sights. There were crowds of people everywhere and the voices all sounded like incoherent mumbling. I couldn't keep my eyes focused on one thing between the little side stores with sales clerks clicking buttons and the people walking by in fast herds. We were taken aside and assisted in filling out a lot of paperwork. None of us could read or understand English, and the translator spoke broken Chinese with a slightly different dialect. Everything felt surreal. I had finally arrived in America, the place I had prayed for and dreamed about all those nights in the workers' camp in Cambodia.

Our second flight ended at Charlotte International Airport in North Carolina on July 10, 1979. Reverend Worth Sweet, the pastor of the church, whom we later grew to call "Pappy Sweet" and Jennie Hightower, a church member, greeted us with big smiles and warm hugs. We were ecstatic to have made it to the place we would soon make our new home in the United States.

Pappy Sweet tried to get us all into a van, but none of us understood what was happening because we had never seen a van before. It was a complete culture shock for everyone involved. We had travelled on two planes and flown for nearly an entire day. With all of the overwhelming changes in our surroundings, we were exhausted and jetlagged.

The van had sliding doors on both sides. Pappy Sweet walked into the van and pointed to the seats, but we still didn't understand that we were supposed to sit down to go for a ride. Then he stepped out the other side of the van after showing us the seats, and we all followed him. It took at least 30 minutes just to get us to understand that we were supposed to stay inside the van. I can't remember how many times we walked in circles around that van. Pappy Sweet was a very patient man and enlisted Jennie's help to stop us from exiting the van after he did.

Finally we sat down, and Jennie and Pappy Sweet were able to get us buckled into our seatbelts. I think they must have been dumbfounded and stunned themselves to be around a family who not only spoke no English, but also didn't even understand the concept of riding in a van.

They drove the van from the airport to a burger restaurant because they knew that we must have been hungry. We sat down at a table and Pappy Sweet set a burger in front of each of us. He had one of his own. He took off the top bun, squeezed some red stuff from a bottle onto the burger in a circular motion, and mashed the top bun back down. He looked up at us with big eyes, took a huge bite of the burger, and said, "Mmm—mm!" He was trying to get us to understand that burgers were food and that we were supposed to eat them, but we were still a little uncertain. He told us to do exactly as he did and so I took the top bun off my burger, grabbed the bottle of red stuff that I later realized was called ketchup, and squeezed way too much on top of the patty. I mashed the top bun down on my burger, took a big bite, and repeated, "Mmm—mm!" just the way Pappy Sweet did. He and Jennie laughed and laughed. In the restaurant we noticed that Pappy Sweet was drinking some kind of brown beverage, and my family thought it was beer or some type of alcohol. It surprised us that the pastor of the church was drinking alcohol. It wasn't until much later that we realized he was drinking iced tea instead of alcohol.

———∞∞∞———

As we became adjusted to living in America, there were many things we didn't understand because they were new to us. We never owned a washing machine or had anything like that in Cambodia. We had to use a Laundromat to wash our clothes after we moved to

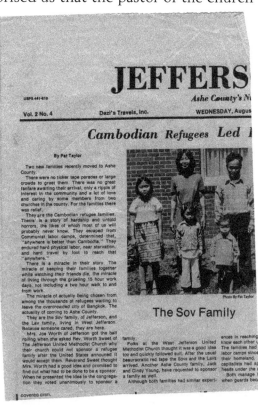

**JEFFERS**

USPS 441-610     Ashe County's N
Vol. 2 No. 4     Dezi's Travels, Inc.     WEDNESDAY, Augus

**Cambodian Refugees Led**

By Pat Taylor

Two new families recently moved to Ashe County.

There were no ticker tape parades or large crowds to greet them. There was no great fanfare awaiting their arrival, only a ripple of interest in the community and a lot of love and caring by some members from two churches in the county. For the families there was relief.

They are the Cambodian refugee families. Theirs is a story of hardship and untold horrors, the likes of which most of us will probably never know. They escaped from Communist labor camps, determined that, "anywhere is better than Cambodia." They endured hard physical labor, near starvation, and hard travel by foot to reach that "anywhere."

There is a miracle in their story. The miracle of keeping their families together while watching their friends die, the miracle of living through the grueling 15 hour work days, not including a two hour walk to and from work.

The miracle of actually being chosen from among the thousands of refugees waiting to leave the overcrowded city of Bangkok. The actuality of coming to Ashe County.

They are the Sov family, of Jefferson, and the Lav family, living in West Jefferson. Because someone cared, they are here.

Mrs. Joe Worth of Jefferson got the ball rolling when she asked Rev. Worth Sweet of the Jefferson United Methodist Church why their church could not sponsor a refugee family after the United States announced it would accept them. Reverend Sweet thought Mrs. Worth had a good idea and promised to find out what had to be done to be a sponsor. When he presented the idea to the congregation they voted unanimously to sponsor a

family.

Folks at the West Jefferson United Methodist Church thought it was a good idea too and quickly followed suit. After the usual beaurocratic red tape the Sovs and the Lavs arrived. Another Ashe County family, Jack and Cindy Young, have requested to sponsor a family as well.

Although both families had similar experi-

ences in reaching
know each other c
The families had
labor camps since
their homeland.
Both manage t
when guards beca

Photo By Pat Taylor

**The Sov Family**

covered dish.

the United States. We walked there one day because it was close to our home and carried our clothes into the Laundromat. We didn't understand how to use a washing machine. It was all new to us and blew our minds. We watched closely what other people were doing and then tried to do exactly what they were doing. We loaded the washing machine, but we were confused when nothing happened. Other people's machines were making noises and going around in circles, but our machine wasn't working. We couldn't figure out what we were doing wrong. A kind couple came into the Laundromat and noticed that we were struggling to use the machine. The woman came over to us and showed us how to put in a quarter and push the buttons to make the machine go. We did what she did and at first inserted two quarters. I didn't understand how much money to put in, so I kept putting quarters into the machine. I thought it was like a little game. The woman who had been helping us came over and said, "No more!" She stopped us from putting any more money into the washing machine and started it for us.

It took us a few tries, but eventually we were able to understand how to use the machines.

"If you falter in a time of trouble,
how small is your strength!"
Proverbs 24:10
(NIV)

## Chapter 2
## *The Life I Didn't Expect*

D ishes were being thrown at me. Wow, I was able to duck down and barely miss the edge of a ceramic plate being hurled at me through the air by my own father-in-law. I thought to myself, *"If this is the better life living in America, I don't want it."* Then a quote came to mind and made me remember that God will make a person try many times. Job 6:11—"What strength do I have, that I should still hope? What prospects, that I should be patient?" (NIV) It was then when I realized that I should be grateful for what God had given me and that I should be patient and know that God would do His work in time.

The first years after I married Kenny in 1991, I thought a young married couple would live happily ever after. But that wasn't the case. We had just moved from Johnson City, Tennessee, to Hamptonville, North Carolina. The loss of my job in Tennessee was unbearable to me because I had never lost a job since I had been able to work after I came to America. That was the only job I've ever lost. The distress was so intense that I had a miscarriage during my first year living with my father-in-law, Kenneth Ashley, at his home. Kenny had thought it would be best for us to live with his father until we could afford a place of our own. He had also thought it would be a good idea to move into Kenneth's house because he had just lost Kenny's mother the year before. We had discussed this move at length and thought it might help his father. We determined that we might be able to keep him company.

***From left to right:***
Sharon Duvall, our pastor's
wife Rachel Sweet,
me, my mother (my biological
aunt), Jennie Hightower,
Dot Colvard

Kenny and Me

Later on in 1993, we were able to build a basement home, and Kenny and I moved there.

For the first three years in our home, we owned a small restaurant near Highway 77 in Jonesville, North Carolina, that we named the Copper Kettle. We served home-style country food for breakfast, lunch, and dinner. The building was already there and we rented it. The restaurant was fairly big; we could seat around 130 people. We hired a kitchen and wait staff. Business was good and I was able to get a job at Unifi while owning the restaurant. The job at Unifi was great because it provided us with health insurance. During this time Kenny and I were making good money, but I had lost my will to serve God and never mentioned Him to anyone. I was noticing a change in my life.

I became pregnant with our daughter Tia and the doctor put me on bed rest due to my previous miscarriage. Because of that, I only spent around six months working at Unifi before they laid me off temporarily. I remained on bed rest for the rest of my pregnancy and gave birth to a healthy, beautiful baby girl in 1994. It was difficult having a newborn baby and being on bed rest because it made it hard for me to hold and feed her. Since it was hard for me to even hold my baby, it caused me distress during those meaningful times when mother-baby bonding is so important.

Not long after having Tia and right after I was relieved from bed rest, I returned to work at Unifi as well as at the restaurant. Kenny and the rest of the restaurant staff needed the help. I worked as a server while my newborn rested in her carriage at a side table in the back of the restaurant. During times when Tia was in the restaurant, other waitresses would help bottle feed her. They'd walk swiftly to her table and latch the bottle in her mouth, letting her drink until she was satisfied. Then they'd quickly continue working. I was beginning to wear down both physically and emotionally from all the stress and from the effort of taking care of Tia and working. I thought, *"This is not the life for me."*

After some deliberation, Kenny and I decided to sell the restaurant. But my life was still in the fast lane and not serving God I even had a preacher, Nat Thompson, come to the restaurant in an attempt to get me to come back to the Swan Creek Baptist Church, but I refused. My excuse was that I was too busy, and it wasn't a lie. Kenny and I worked from morning until late night every day. Kenny's dad was helping with the restaurant until we could leave, and then he would leave once everything was finished.

Then one day, my father-in-law was at my house visiting from 3:00 in the afternoon until 8:30, when I got off work. I was feeling stressed from my long day and waiting for Kenny to get out of the

shower, which he did around nine. And I was becoming frustrated that at that point my father-in-law was still at my house. At the time I was once again working at Unifi, a manufacturing company, on first shift. Kenny also worked there on third shift. Kenny and I switched off taking care of our daughter Tia because we didn't have anyone to watch her. This was not good for either one of us.

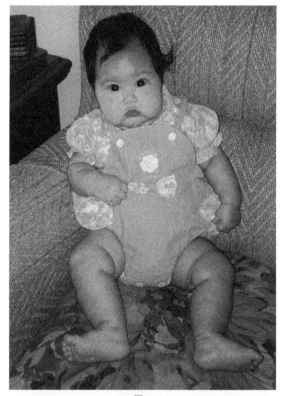

Tia

Kenny and I were incredibly busy and it was taking a toll on me. I continued to push forward the best I could, but every day was a struggle for me from the time I woke up until the time I went to bed.

" 'For I know the plans I have for you,'
declares the Lord, 'plans for welfare and
not for evil, to give you a future and a hope.' "
Jeremiah 29:11
(ESV)

# Chapter 3
## *Memories of School*

T here was one day that I can remember more vividly than others: my first day of school in kindergarten in America. I was 13 years old when school started in August 1979 and I turned 14 in September. I remember lining up for lunch in the cafeteria and being amazed by all the food. I had never seen so much food at one time, and all of it looked different from anything I was used to eating in Cambodia. I can still see the little elementary-school children lining up to get food at the school, and so I followed them. There was one little boy named Matt Sheets who was in my class. He was much smaller than me and stood next to me in the lunch line. Due to my age, *everyone* was smaller than I was, and it felt a bit strange being so much bigger than all the other kids.

At the time I didn't even know what a milk carton was, but I was happy to receive it. The cafeteria staff gave me a tray of food, and I took it and sat down at one of the long cafeteria tables. I remember having green beans, mashed potatoes, Salisbury steak with gravy, a fruit cup, a cookie, and a rice-crispy treat. I didn't know what any of the foods were. I began to devour my food with my hands, just as I would've done in Cambodia. I looked up from my plate and the kids were all staring at me as if I were doing something wrong. My teacher unwrapped the plastic on a set of plastic cutlery for me and took out the fork, the spoon, and a little butter knife. Then the kids started to show me how to use the eating utensils. It was my very first lesson at school. After the kids showed me how to use my fork and spoon and how to cut my steak, we all finished our lunches.

Then we started to get up from the table. I thought we could go back through the line and get more food, so that's what I did. I didn't know any better. The cafeteria staff let me eat an extra plate of food that first day, probably because they could see how starved I had been.

In the school days that followed, I learned that I was only allowed to have one tray of food for lunch. I was thankful to the other kids for showing me how to eat properly with my fork, spoon, and knife. And I was thankful to the cafeteria staff who fed us at the school. Everything was different from what I was used to in Cambodia, but I took it all in stride and adjusted as well as I could.

Another time at school the janitor was cleaning the floor. I was sitting at the table with the other children working on my homework. He was trying to explain to me how to throw away trash. He picked up a piece of paper that was loose on the floor, crumpled it up in a ball, and threw it in the trashcan. He was trying to help me understand, but I still didn't quite catch on. I followed his lead and promptly completed my homework, crumpled it up in a ball, and threw it away! After a few times when I had thrown out my homework, the teacher realized what I was doing. It took her several times to explain to me the difference between good work that was to be kept and turned in to the teacher and incorrect work and other trash that can be thrown away. The teacher demonstrated this to me on a piece of paper by intentionally making a mistake and throwing away the paper. She said, "This is bad. It is trash." On another piece of paper, she filled it out as it was supposed to be completed and said, "This one is good. We keep it." She set that paper on the table in a stack of its own. It took her a few times of her showing this to me before I understood the concept and realized that I'd been throwing all my good work away.

I didn't understand what a bathroom was or how to use it. The other kids would go into the bathroom, and I would just stare at what was going on and try to figure out what people were doing. I noticed that a girl would go into the bathroom and then go into a stall. Then I would hear a little "swoosh" sound and she would come out. I went into my own stall and used the toilet. But I had no idea what toilet paper was used for, and I was scared to close the stall door. In Cambodia, we used a scoop of water to rinse off after using the bathroom. Toilet paper does not exist in Cambodia. A little girl, a kindergartner, came up to my stall. She looked almost appalled to see me stand up and not know what to do. I was looking around for a scoop and pail of water, but there wasn't one to be found. She took toilet paper off the roll, rolled it up on her hand, and showed me how to use it to wipe. I had a little child showing me how to properly use the restroom, but I didn't know any better and I'm glad that she did.

I had all these wonderful teachers who were willing to help me learn. It was confusing to be around so many people talking and to be unable to comprehend what was said. It sounded jumbled whenever anyone talked. When a number of people in an entire room talked, it overwhelmed my head with different sounds. I'm sure I looked dumbfounded. It was difficult to understand anything. The first word I remember learning was Pepsi. I remember a teacher holding the glass bottle up and repeating, "Pep-si," until I could repeat it.

Laura McConnell was my kindergarten teacher. She started out teaching me the English alphabet, repeating letters and writing them until I was able to repeat her. I started to understand that certain symbols meant certain sounds. The first book I ever learned how to read was *Run, Spot, Run*. The teacher acted out the words on the page. They had a mat out on the floor and ran across it as if a dog were running. I was so entertained by that, and I loved being able to understand the words. Once I figured out how to read it, I repeated it over and over.

It was such a happy feeling to learn, and I was eager to know more. I wanted to learn as fast as I could. I wanted to get as far as I could and push myself to try my hardest so that I could catch up to the other kids who were my age. Ms. McConnell was a very kind woman, and she was patient working with me on top of teaching all the other children how to read.

Shirley Craven was the assistant kindergarten teacher. She was also very patient and made sure to correct me whenever I made a mistake in trying to write my letters. She worked with me on how to hold the pencil and taught me how to hold it correctly. She guided my hand in the correct place, so I would know for myself how to do it.

Kindergarten was a very important class to me, and I learned a lot in that class.

All the other kindergartners drew pictures at our table. They said each word over and over. Teachers gave out all kinds of paperwork on which we traced dots in order to spell words and create letters and numbers. I particularly remember seeing a picture of a bird with the words "the bird flies" written underneath. There were papers with blank sections where the other kindergartners were fast at filling in the blanks with the correct words. I was struggling to form letters and understand the associations between the pictures and the words.

All the other kindergartners were wonderful. They knew that I was much bigger than them. I was big, but not yet educated. They were eager to help an older kid. I'm sure they all felt special being able to help a big kid learn and being able to understand something that an older kid was having a much harder time understanding. I was especially fond of Matt Sheets, who always wanted to help me, even in the lunch line.

Ly Huor Sov (my cousin who was now my sister) was in my kindergarten class too, but she started at the age of six. The teachers had to be more concentrated on my learning. Ly went through school like any normal child due to her age, so the teachers' urgency to work with her was far less. The teachers knew that they had far less precious time to teach me all I needed to learn. I needed to learn fast in order to catch up to the other children and to finish school.

Willa Campbell was my math teacher. In comparison to reading, math was a lot easier for me to learn. But the language barrier made it a little difficult until I learned to adapt. Once I learned English words, it made it easy for me to learn numbers. Numbers just made sense to me.

Every day I went to kindergarten for a couple of hours, then to first grade for a couple of hours, and then to second grade for a couple of hours. Mary Gordon Tugman was my second-grade teacher. She even taught me how to eat broccoli. Mrs. Tugman insisted that I eat broccoli, but I didn't want to because it looked like little trees and it freaked me out. She acted like she was going to scold me once because I refused to eat it, but she never spanked me or anything like that. I remember standing in the lunch line and having her put that green stuff on my plate. I know I must've looked disgusted. The thought of eating little trees bothered me, but I learned to eat it. I ate the broccoli and to this day, I love it.

Mrs. Tugman made sure that I was doing everything properly and took her time to teach me even though I was much bigger than the rest of the kids. She also went to church with me, so I got to spend extra time with her learning about God.

Kindergarten

Grade
School
Awards

Mr. Bruce Roten was my sixth-grade teacher. He made sure I could write English properly. He had a ruler and he would pop you on the hand with it when you made an error.

Gale Hurley was the principal and he checked on me in class with all my teachers from time to time. It seemed as though every time he came around, the teacher would have more work for me to do, so Mr. Hurley really pushed me to learn. But I didn't have a problem with him or with more work. I wanted more to do. I wanted to learn *everything*.

My favorite physical-education teacher was Mr. Eddie Byers. He made sure I would play with the other kids. We played jump rope together and practiced tossing a ball back and forth. We played Red Rover, which it took me a while to understand. We also got to go outdoors and use the playground swings.

I learned a lot at church too. I remember seeing people in robes and not understanding why they had to wear them. The people opened up the Bible and preached. I looked at the book and didn't know what it was until I heard the word *Jesus*. Then I jumped up out of my seat ecstatically because I had heard that word before. It wasn't until about six months after I was in the United States that Pappy Sweet realized I had heard of Jesus before through my father's trips to the capital of Cambodia. Pappy Sweet was a good person, just like everyone else whom I grew up so quickly around.

I remember being the acolyte at the church. Like most other things, it was new to my family and we were not sure what we were doing. The first time I saw someone being the acolyte, I thought, *"Wow,"* because it was neat seeing all those candles lit. They passed us our hymnbooks. Though we didn't understand the words, we hummed along with everyone else who was singing. It was very different for us being around that type of music. And it sounded beautiful the way everyone's voices and the organ filled the room with song.

Once—close to the beginning of when we started going to church—I remember seeing a flag symbol that I recognized from the uniform worn by the soldier who saved me from the mountaintop in Cambodia. I was really excited and wanted so badly to tell someone that I had seen that flag before, but I didn't know how to say it. I saw the same flag again at school in our kindergarten classroom. There I stood with the other kindergartners when saying the Pledge of Allegiance, put my hand over my heart, and tried to speak like they did. But the words took a while for me to learn. At that time, we also said a prayer as a class. It was a good way to bring us all together and make us feel connected. It helped shape my understanding of community and American culture.

Each day when I got home from school, it was as if my learning stalled. I really didn't get much out of being at home except for being able to be with my family. My parents couldn't speak English at all, so I had to speak Chinese to communicate with them, while still trying to keep everything I learned at school fresh and in my head. Each day when I got back to school, I had to remember how to speak English again.

I really couldn't wait to go to school every day. It was always something different, fun, and new. And I loved it.

"And the God of all grace, who called you
to His eternal glory in Christ, after you have
suffered a little while, will Himself restore you
and make you strong, firm and steadfast."
1 Peter 5:10
(NIV)

## Chapter 4

# *Things Begin to Decline*

In 2004 my father-in-law, Kenneth Ashley, came to my house and told me he wanted to see the doctor because his big toe on his right foot had become infected. I agreed to take him. When I took him there, the doctor said that the toe would need to be amputated due to gangrene. We had to come back the next day to have the toe removed.

After the amputation, I went to his house every day and made sure that he was doing okay. I had to unwrap and fix his bandage and make sure that the wound stayed clean, but he was in a lot of pain. Things weren't getting any better, so we took him back to the doctor, and the news wasn't good. The foot wasn't healing like it needed to and the infection had spread. Kenneth wasn't properly managing his diabetes. Because of that, he had to have his entire right foot amputated in 2005. I had to continue to clean the wound every day and make sure that he took his medicine so the gangrene wouldn't spread any farther. It was a nightmare.

We eventually limited our time to checking on him every once in a while over the course of the next year. But unfortunately, he began consuming alcohol more frequently, which caused more problems for him. He was an alcoholic.

He started to hurt again, so we took him to the doctor again. The doctor said that things weren't good and that he wasn't well. The doctor told us that his leg would need to be removed below the knee, which he didn't want. We didn't want it either. We had no choice—despite trying to figure out other options—but to have his right leg amputated up to his knee in 2006.

When we took Kenneth back to his home after he was released from the hospital, we had a problem. His house wasn't handicap accessible. We either had to remodel his house and find a live-in nurse or move him in with us and help take care of him. Kenny thought it would be too much of a burden on me to have his father in our home all the time. But I made the difficult decision that our home was the best place for him, so we moved him in with us.

With Tia and Ty growing up when I made this big decision, I knew that it would be a lot to manage. I also had my husband to take care of, and I had to work. But my father-in-law was family and I knew that he deserved to live somewhere he would be cared for and treated well. I also knew that he wanted to move in with us and that he agreed it would be the better choice. Though Kenny didn't agree with my decision, he went along with it because he understood that it was the best decision for all of us. I'm sure Kenny thought at some point, *"How hard can it be to take care of another person?"* It can be *very difficult,* as I was to learn in the following years.

After his leg was amputated, my father-in-law had to have rehabilitation therapy at Forsyth Memorial Hospital in Winston-Salem. Kenneth and I went there every day. The therapist worked with him and taught him how to get up and down out of his wheelchair. The rehabilitation therapist helped him gain some strength back in his muscles to support himself.

It was a constant challenge for me to manage everything. The

36

first year that my father-in-law moved in, he tried to listen. But he cheated any chance he could get. He ate what he wasn't supposed to all the time. *How was I supposed to separate the food for him and for my family?* I came home from my waitressing job to prepare the food to feed the whole family and found food missing from the refrigerator. Kenneth had eaten it, and it wasn't meant for him. I couldn't figure out how I was supposed to separate the food.

During this point in my life, I still continued my path without church and I was almost going insane. I had too much going on at once and was concerned about everyone. I wasn't being good to my children or to my father-in-law. I yelled at everyone, and I didn't realize the toll it was all taking on me. I raised my voice all the time, and I got so frustrated with everyone. I just wanted things to go smoothly, and I wanted everything to go well. I had also dealt with post-traumatic stress disorder for years, and the stressors caused by juggling everything in my life at that time caused the PTSD to be worse as well. At that point, God was still not on my mind. I prayed, but my prayers were full of anger and God knows that. There were reasons why that time in my life was very stressful and full of strife. It was largely because of the lack of my relationship with God. God put me through many trials before my complete faith in Him would be restored.

It was a daily hardship taking care of Kenneth. I got up at six in the morning and got breakfast ready for my kids and my father-in-law. They ate different things, so I made two meals. I got them up at seven and let the kids eat their breakfast. My father-in-law ate his special meal. I got the kids cleaned up and dressed to get them ready for school. Then I told my father-in-law I was leaving, and I left and took Tia and Ty to school. By the time I got back home, it was right after eight o'clock. I cleaned and straightened up the house. I tried to get Kenneth to go sit outdoors in his wheelchair and get some sunshine. After I was finished with the cleaning, I spent a little time with him outdoors and then fixed lunch and served him food. After that, I went to the grocery store, got the kids from school around 2:30 P.M., and helped them do their homework. By 5:00 in the afternoon, I had dinner cooked and ready and served everyone food. I got the kids washed up and ready for bed. After 11:00 each night, I had just a little bit of time to spend with Kenny. That was my schedule for Monday through Friday, every single day.

In addition to taking care of everything at home, I was also working as a substitute teacher for Yadkin County Schools during any spare time I had. During each weekend, I worked as a waitress at a restaurant. On Saturdays, I went in around 10:30 in the morning and got off at 4:00. I went in on Sunday afternoons—after church around 4:00—and I would get off around 11. That was exhausting too.

Providing for my children and for Kenneth took a major toll on my faith and well-being. Kenneth totally depended on me and treated me as though I were his wife. I wasn't a replacement for her, and I couldn't sustain his happiness. It's apparent to me, even now, that people throughout the community thought I was married to Kenneth. The doctor thought he was my husband at first. I saw people out and about around town who were under the same impression. It was a challenge to take care of so much at the same time. I wasn't only worried about myself. I had to put everyone else and their needs before my own. I wasn't getting enough sleep at night, my meals were rushed and focused on making sure that everyone else was eating properly, and I was completely drained from trying to keep track of everyone's schedule. I didn't have any friends to turn to for support during this time in my life. I had Kenny—whom I barely saw—and my young children who relied on me to provide for them. I left God out of the equation. I wasn't thinking about Him and felt cynical toward Him when I did think about Him. It was a very difficult time in my life.

I had thought that everything in America would be perfect. Although I wasn't in Cambodia any longer, that time in my life was the first time since I'd been in Cambodia when I had felt so down. Even when I lived in Cambodia, I had felt like I had a purpose, which was to make it to America as my dad told me to do all those years ago. During the time when I cared for Kenneth, I had forgotten about the faith that I held so dear in the Cambodian workers' camp. Faith in God was my saving grace, and it seemed farther away from me than ever.

During the second year of taking care of Kenny's father, I realized that I had to get back in touch with God. At that point in my life, I was so down that I was looking for help from anybody willing to help, but I didn't have anyone. I even asked Kenneth's brother and sister if they could take him every once in a while to do things. But they didn't take him because they either couldn't or wouldn't. I decided to pray and said, "God, this is it. It's just You and me. You are the one who gave me the voice to let Kenneth in and bring him into this house, and I need help."

In the third year of taking care of Kenneth, he had to have a pacemaker put in. He had already had a quadruple bypass many years before that. After getting the pacemaker in early 2007, he did well for several months. The doctors told him to exercise and we tried to keep him active. But he didn't want to be active. He had a prosthetic leg that he was supposed to wear so he could be active. I went to physical therapy with him and tried to walk with him. Each time after he got home from therapy, he removed his prosthetic leg, and he sat and did nothing despite my advice. Kenny and I tried to get him to do things, but he refused. I don't think a lot of people realize how draining and time consuming it is to take care of an elderly person. It requires a lot of sacrifice.

After Kenneth had remained inactive for a while, his other leg—his left one—began hurting. We took him to the hospital and he remained there for a week. The doctors told us that the best option was to amputate his left leg. At first the doctor wanted to try again as they had the first time on his right leg and amputate his left leg piece by piece, chopping it off as and if needed. I said I wasn't going to let them chop him up like that again. I asked the doctor which choice would be the most helpful, and he said it would probably do more good to amputate the leg above the knee. Kenneth, Kenny, and I had to make the tough decision to have the left leg amputated above the knee instead of at the knee. This time, the medical team did the full amputation of his leg in late 2007. It took nearly three months for Kenneth to heal and get back to normal. When the doctor sent him home, I had to examine the wound and dress it. But at that point, I was able to get a nurse to come in every day while I was at work and look after him. That was really helpful.

As our kids got older, they had after-school and extracurricular activities that they attended. I had to take them to cheerleading and ball practice. I never really was able to get a break, and I didn't get any time to myself.

Kenny and I struggled with our relationship a great deal during this time. We weren't able to have any time alone. We were always overworked, exhausted, and cranky. I felt like I was smothering inside my own home where every day was a constant chore and my relationships with those around me became tedious. I couldn't maintain the intimacy my marriage needed because we had no privacy at all between Kenneth and the kids.

Kenneth Ashley, Sr.

"For the Lord gives wisdom; from his mouth come knowledge and understanding."
Proverbs 2:6
(NIV)

## Chapter 5
### Flashback to a Better Time

I often think about when I first arrived in America and how excited I was at the prospect of getting an education. Memories of this time almost grew to haunt me as I went through the trials of growing up, becoming an adult, and taking on more responsibility. I'm still proud and impressed with how well I did after first arriving in the United States. I think about how I came here from a background where we had no formal education and illiteracy was common. I was incredibly eager to learn and I wanted to know as much as I could about America because I wanted to be an American more than anything in the world. My father had inspired me from an early age to learn about American life and had known that my freedom and life depended on coming here.

During my first year of schooling, I completed kindergarten through fifth grade. I started school in August 1979 at Jefferson Elementary School, which was a kindergarten through eighth-grade school. They rotated classes around for me so that I could learn as much as possible in order for me to pass and learn how to read, do math, and have an understanding of basic social studies and American subjects.

During the second year of my education (1980–81), I completed sixth grade. In sixth grade, I started going to the reading program a lot and things began to make sense in my mind a little better. The more books I picked out and attempted to read, the more I understood about American culture and how people in the United States lived. I was curious about everything and read anything I could. As soon as I finished reading one book, I turned it in and checked out another one. I earned a certificate for reading that was very special to me. I spent a lot of time checking out books and it paid off!

One of Many
Reading Certificates

I completed seventh grade in my third year of school (1981–82). Most of seventh grade was preparation for the rest of my education.

Eighth grade also took an entire year for me to complete and it was my fourth year in school (1982–83). I was very excited because I was going to attend a different school after completing that year. I continued to work hard, passing every test that I could just so I could make it to the bigger high school. I didn't have a chance to do much of anything other than studying. When I was at home, I helped babysit and take care of the kids, so I didn't have a lot of time to myself or time to do much with friends. It took me longer to complete my eighth-grade year because I had to be 100 percent ready for high school. There was more that I had to prepare for, and my teachers and the principal wanted me to be confident and know what to expect.

During my fifth year of school (1983–84), I completed my freshman year. I completed my sophomore year in my sixth year of school (1984–85). That was very difficult. It was a complete overload of educational material and learning. I was in high school at Ashe Central High School, which no longer exists. We were the Panthers. Wow, it was totally different from kindergarten through eighth grade. I was in a different school, and there was more freedom. People were suddenly bigger and I was around kids closer to my own age. I met a lot of different friends while in high school. That was my first time in school when I actually had time to go out and hang out with friends.

We went to basketball games and I didn't understand the game at all. I couldn't even grasp that the ball "jumped" from one end of the court to another. I just knew that the bouncing motion was entertaining to me. I didn't understand the concepts of the game, the purpose of the net, and why those men were running around. It was amazing to me to experience those games. We didn't have toys and sports like that in Cambodia. I kept finding myself away from my seat and my friend Mitzi would have to find me. I'd have walked all the way down the bleachers and almost onto the basketball court trying to get a closer look at the game. Mitzi had to explain that I didn't know any better, but I think it was funny to her.

I also went to a college-tournament basketball game and by

chance met Michael Jordan and the entire University of North Carolina basketball team! I didn't know whom he was, but apparently it was a big deal to everyone else, so I was excited right along with them. The year was 1984. My friend Mitzi Walker took me to the game. Michael Jordan asked me if I'd like his autograph, and I didn't even know what an autograph was. He had to go and find a pen himself because I didn't have one. He was very nice. It took me years after that before I finally understood whom he was and just how lucky I was to get his autograph. Matt Doherty and some of the other team members on the University of North Carolina Tar Heels team signed their autographs as well. After that game, I wanted to keep going back to more basketball games.

Carolina Tarheels Basketball Team Photo—1984

During my sophomore year of high school, my girlfriends decided to sign me up for the Miss Ashe County pageant without telling me. I went to a meeting about the pageant and ended up getting sponsored to participate. I can't remember where my dress for the main event came from, but I probably borrowed it from a friend. There was so much going on that I didn't even notice a themed backdrop on the stage. I was focused on following what I was supposed to do and enjoying myself. When I've looked back at photographs, I recognized that it was an under-the-sea themed event. They had even created tags with our numbers on them that looked like little fish. I was contestant number five.

The dress I wore was long and white with red, embroidered trim. It came down to a V-neckline in the front and there were little flowers sewn into the material. I wore white heels underneath that could barely be seen due to the length of the dress. I remember a friend, Jesse, helping me get ready for the pageant. She fixed my

hair, and it looked beautiful curling around my shoulders. She put makeup on me, including mascara and bright-red lipstick.

My pageant talent was playing my guitar and singing "Frankie and Johnny." Mr. Roten and some of my other teachers had all pitched in to buy a guitar as a Christmas gift for me, and I had learned how to play it. For

my talent performance, I wore simple cropped jeans, black-and-white shoes, and a light button-up blouse. Jesse put my hair up so it wouldn't be in my face as I sat on a stool onstage, played my guitar, and sang into the microphone.

There was a swimsuit event too. I wore my white shoes with a more conservative one-piece bathing suit. The bathing suit was pink and white striped with a skinny, patent-leather white belt at the waist. I was really scared. There were many pageant rules about how you walked, where you stood, and that you always had to smile.

I didn't know what I was doing. I just followed everyone else. I remember the audience laughing and clapping. They were probably laughing at me, but I didn't have a care in the world because it was so much fun being onstage. It made me feel even more like an American getting to participate and see all the smiling faces. I ended up being in the top ten. At the end of the pageant, I was awarded with a sash that read "Non-Finalist Talent."

One of my best friends in high school, Mitzi Walker, went to Northwest Ashe High School but spent some time with me at my school because her mother worked in the library. She also spent time teaching me how to do things. She taught me how to ride a bicycle. One day we took the bicycle and were riding down a very steep hill that was about a mile long. She encouraged me to ride by saying, "You can do it, Siv!" I listened to her and took off down the hill. I forgot to press the brake down and the bike started to move too fast. I wrecked and scraped my knee. But I learned how to ride it my very first try.

In my seventh year of school, I skipped the junior year and finally completed my senior year (1985–86). I was able to graduate. That was a difficult seven years of education and I felt so accomplished when everything was finished. I was very proud of myself.

I had joined the DECA Club, which is Distributive Education Clubs of America. That enabled me to develop working skills while still continuing to go to school. DECA prepares emerging leaders and entrepreneurs in marketing, finance, hospitality, and management. Harold Phipps was my English teacher and he had given us the assignment of writing a brief autobiography. He read this short description of my personal history and was amazed. He sent my short autobiography in to the DECA magazine. They published my article alongside a story of a refugee from Vietnam in the January/February 1986 edition of *New Dimensions— An Official Publication of the Distributive Education Clubs of America.* (Since then, the DECA magazine has been renamed. It's now called *DECA Dimensions.*) I couldn't believe that they picked my article. I was so excited. I knew that what I learned would contribute to my understanding and appreciation of the

An Official Publication of the Distributive Education Clubs of America **NEW** January/February 1986

# DIMENSI◆NS

$1.25

## the DECA IMAGE

## National IMAGE

DECA Creed Has Special Meaning

The DECA Creed states, "I believe in the future which I am planning for myself . . . I believe in fulfilling the highest measure of service to my vocation, my fellow beings, my country and my God . . . I believe in the democratic philosophies . . . and in the freedoms of this nation . . . ."

Many times we state the DECA Creed but what we say are words without meaning. The Creed has special meaning for two members of DECA at the Ashe County Career Center, West Jefferson, North Carolina. An Ngoc Vo is a refugee from Vietnam and Siv Lang Sov is a refugee from Cambodia. Freedom has a special meaning to these two DECA members. When they recite the DECA Creed they mean what they say. Their stories follow:

Pictured left, Siv Lang Sov and An Ngoc Vo

My name is An Ngoc Vo. I am originally from Vietnam. I was a spy for my father who went underground after the American military pulled out of Vietnam. When I was discovered I escaped by small boat with several of my fellow countrymen. While at sea the boat was continually attacked by pirates. I finally made my escape to Thailand. Six years ago I came to the United States. I came here for various reasons, but mainly for freedom, the freedom that the United States offers that no other country has.

My family's chosen occupation was that of restaurant marketing, and as a result I have learned a great many things about this area of business. My goal is to become a successful restaurant owner.

I believe this is the place where I can make my dream come true. Here in the United States I have the

I cannot put into words my deep appreciation for all the generosity which has been shown to me by so many Americans. Presently I am living with adopted parents in Jefferson, North Carolina, and am enrolled in marketing education at the Ashe County Career Center. Last year I was a junior and discovered DECA. I was elected president of my junior class Chapter and from that experience I have gained a new meaning of education. The marketing education class and DECA has inspired me and offered me a challenge and opportunities to develop good leadership qualities.

This year I am a senior and again president of my Chapter. I am currently a candidate for district president. I believe my future has begun in DECA.

After I graduate from high school, I plan to attend Appalachian State University and major in marketing education.

From the bottom of my heart, I am glad to be a member of DECA and I am honored to serve my fellow DECA members as president. I am very proud to be here on United States soil and within three months I will be a citizen of this great country.

My name is Siv Lang Sov. I was born on September 18, 1965, in a land of great beauty called Cambodia. I was

parents were killed. It was about two years later that I was on my own searching for a place called America. There were many, many mountains that I had to travel through. It took days and nights to walk across the mountains. I had to climb trees to get food and I also killed animals to eat.

Four years later I landed in Thailand. American people had sent food and supplies to the refugees. It took me about two weeks to come to America by plane. The Jefferson United Methodist Church sponsored me.

Six years have passed since I was thirteen years old and started in school at Jefferson Elementary School in Jefferson, North Carolina. Things were very difficult then, and I have moved from kindergarten to the eleventh grade in six years.

Now I am a junior and will be able to graduate this spring. I am presently in DECA. I have been elected president of my junior class Chapter. I am learning that the purpose of DECA is to develop a respect for education in marketing. I know that what I learn will contribute to my vocational competence and will promote my understanding and appreciation for the responsibilities of citizenship in our free, competitive enterprise system. Being involved in marketing education has made me aware of opportunities open to me in marketing, merchandising and management. I am also learning how to better develop myself socially and professionally by working on my job after school and "learning by doing."

I have learned a lot and I wish for all students to know that DECA members serve as leaders and as team members. We strive to b...

responsibilities of living and working in America, and I took any new opportunity presented to me.

I was also in the French Club, so I was trying to learn another language in addition to being new at speaking the English language.

I took French to meet a high-school language requirement. It was really difficult for me to grasp, but I did it. I was also a representative on the Student Council and I eventually was elected the president of the junior-class chapter of the DECA Club.

Miss Linda Lindsey was a teacher for writer studies in deep reading. I read a lot in that class. By the time I finished her reading course, I had read more than 100 books and had received numerous awards for reading achievement. She helped me every day with studying, and her assistance really helped me accomplish more of my goals.

I received rewards often in school. Teachers gave me a little certificate every time I completed reading 25 books. I must have a dozen of those certificates, though most of the books I read were short ones and I favored books related to animals most of all. I thought it was fun to learn about all of the world's different creatures. As I went farther along in my education, the books I read became longer and more detailed. I won an award for poetry a little later in my schooling, and it made me feel proud to have others enjoy reading something I had written. I also received an award for perfect attendance in high school, but I was serious about being there to learn, and I wanted to be present.

The Ashe County Career Center presented me with an award for Marketing Education on June 4, 1986. I was also granted a scholarship from

DECA's North Carolina association in 1986 to attend Wilkes Community College. Later I went on to make the dean's list at Wilkes Community College. I developed a concept of "learning by

doing" early on, and I've carried this ideology everywhere since.

⸻

I started to study for my American citizenship. I had an attorney through Bill and Morning Lopp in Jefferson, and they helped me learn the laws and the history. I was going through the education process so quickly that I really needed more instruction about what I needed to learn in order to pass the test to obtain my citizenship. Finally, in 1985, I was sworn in as a citizen of the United States of America.

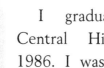

I graduated from Ashe Central High School in 1986. I was invited to give a presentation to the North Carolina Association of Educators instructional workshop that year. I gave a speech at their event about how students view change and also discussed coming to Ashe County as a Cambodian refugee.

During my first year in school, I realized how hard I had to work and how hard all the teachers worked to help me. I made a lot of progress in a short amount of time. Thinking back, it's really incredible how much I was able to learn and how much I improved each day. I knew that if I could accomplish that in this land of opportunity, then it would also give hope to more refugees as well as immigrants. No one ever said it would be easy, and it certainly was a lot of work. But it was worth every bit of the time and effort I spent struggling and studying.

⸻

I started working at Makoto's, a Japanese restaurant in Boone, around September of my senior year in high school. I wanted to keep it a secret from my mother so she wasn't concerned about me messing up my schooling. Later on, after I worked there for a couple of years, my boss thought that I would make an excellent head waitress. I was promoted from head waitress to manager after a year. After my graduation from Wilkes Community College, I was working there full-time. I managed Makoto's for almost two years and my boss bought another restaurant in Johnson City, Tennessee. He eventually came to me and asked if I'd like to move to Johnson City so that he could be closer to his wife and have more time with her, so I transferred to that restaurant and started working there. I had already met Kenny and we had started dating, but it wasn't a big deal for me to travel.

At home with my family, the rest of the kids and I tried to teach our parents what we had learned. We learned small words and then went home and tried to recite the words to our parents in hopes that it would help. It was difficult for our parents to learn English because they weren't submerged in the language the way we kids were.

My father (my uncle) took a job at Leather Goods in Boone, where he worked from around 1980 to 1986 until I suggested to him that he try to get a job working as a chef at Makoto's Japanese restaurant. He still works there to this day.

For a few years living in the United States, our mother (my biological aunt) didn't work. She gave birth to their third and youngest child, Mary, in 1980. After that she got a job working at Hanes Company and worked there for about 25 years. Then she worked for Jefferson Apparel for a couple of years.

Dad, Mom, and Me
Today

*Left to Right:*
Me, Mom,
Ly Huor (in green),
Ly Chou (in pink),
and Dad

Mary Jenny, my youngest
sister, who was born in
Jefferson, North Carolina

As both of Kenny's and my children grew up, I encouraged them to go for it and do whatever it was they wanted to do. Change happens fast and I tried to teach them that the better we adapt to change, the better off we'll be. Those years I spent in Ashe County, it was interesting to observe the changes in the community that went along with changes in local businesses and smaller companies that were being overrun by larger industries.

*Left to Right:*
Tia, Me, Kenny, and Ty

Kenny and Me

"I consider that our present sufferings
are not worth comparing with the glory
that will be revealed in us."
Romans 8:18
(NIV)

## Chapter 6

# *My Living Nightmare*

S uddenly things around me weren't clearly outlined, and I was having trouble figuring out exactly what was happening. I abruptly realized that I had abandoned my disabled brother Maine at the children's work camp in Cambodia! I knew that he was severely injured. I had only random memories of the woman at the pit telling me I had to leave and never turn back. Those fleeting memories quickly came and left. Panicked and sickened at the thought of leaving my own little brother to die, I rushed back to the pit where I had left him. But before I could reach him, there were Red soldiers pulling him away from me. The closer I got to Maine, the farther away the soldiers pulled him from my reach. I was running toward him as fast as I could, screaming for them to let him go. I couldn't see their faces clearly, and I couldn't even tell if it were actually Maine whom they were so intently dragging away from me. My panic increased as the figures became more blurred. I felt such overwhelming agony and heartbreak as the realization hit that Maine was fading away from me, and I could never reach him. Suddenly I saw a bright light in front of me, and I woke up with sweat running down my face.

Reality hit me hard, and I realized that I was standing in the middle of the street. Kenny and others were calling out to me. I was having some kind of night terrors that involved sleepwalking and nightmares. I had gotten out of bed in the middle of the night, and I was literally running down the street barefooted, in my pajamas.

I had kept details about my past a secret from Kenny. I didn't talk much about all of the horror and trauma that I experienced in the Cambodian work camp. Instead I wanted to focus on what was going on in my life in America and block out everything I could from my past. I didn't want anyone to feel sorry for me.

I had night terrors from the time I left Cambodia until well into my marriage. During the sleepwalking and in the bad dreams, I was reliving what I went through in the work camps and leaving my brother who had died before I escaped.

A lot of people ask me if I *regret* not having gone back to save my brother, but *regret* is such a harsh word. I have returned to Cambodia three times, hoping on each trip that I would see a familiar face and find Maine. But I've never found him. I assume that the woman at the pit was truthful and he is dead, but there will always be a part of me that will hold on to that memory. All that I experienced in the Cambodian work camp was a living nightmare. Ever since leaving Cambodia in 1979, I had been living with post-traumatic stress disorder (PTSD). However, at that time, there wasn't much public discourse involving PTSD after the Vietnam War.

I had to get past leaving my brother behind because I couldn't continue to live in regret of something I did as a terrified, 13-year-old child. I did exactly what I had to do to survive. The old woman at the pit in the camp told me to run and get out of there. She insisted that Maine was dead and that I would be dead soon too if I didn't leave right then with the group implementing their escape from the work camp at that very moment. It was a life-or-death situation, and I had to listen to her and run as fast as I could to catch up with the others before I missed out on my last chance to flee.

"And without faith it is impossible
to please God, because anyone who
comes to Him must believe
that He exists and that He rewards
those who earnestly seek Him."
Hebrews 11:6
(NIV)

## Chapter 7
# I Abandon God

The first year that Kenneth stayed with us was very hard. I had to go to work, take my kids to school, pick them up from school, take Tia to cheerleading practice, and then run home and make sure that my father-in-law was okay since he was unable to walk and get around unless he used his prosthetic legs, which he rarely did. I had to cook multiple meals: one pertaining to his diet and another for us. At night, I didn't stop and go to bed until around 11:00 or midnight. I felt rushed and run-down. I was becoming more angry and lonely, and I didn't have anyone to talk with about my feelings because Kenny was working long hours. I had truly lost touch with God and my relationship with Him during this point in my life, and I was beginning to feel lost.

I didn't realize that taking care of my own children and my handicapped father-in-law would be such a problem and so difficult. It was a constant struggle and I hurt every day. I was beginning to get frustrated because Kenny wasn't able to help me in ways I started to feel I needed his help. I asked for help, which I didn't get, and I was starting to look for a way out of my current life and situation. My father-in-law became more and more dependent on me to do every little thing for him. I was distraught and depressed, and I didn't feel hopeful about the future. Once again, post-traumatic stress disorder factored into all my symptoms as I was flagging physically, mentally, and emotionally due to taking care of my father-in-law, husband, and two children.

I was working as a substitute teacher during the earlier time when Kenneth was living with us, and I waited tables on the weekends. I was beyond exhausted. I got to the point that I was so anxious I felt like I couldn't even breathe. By the fifth year of dealing with all of this, I thought that I was going to have to file for divorce. I didn't get to do anything because I didn't have time for anything.

Kenneth continued to live with us until 2011. That year he was diagnosed with kidney failure. Kenneth, Kenny, and I had to work with his doctors to make the decision whether to do surgery on his kidneys or to start Kenneth on kidney dialysis three days every week. We didn't want him to suffer through any more surgeries. Instead he started on kidney dialysis and was on it for about three to four months. About four months after he was diagnosed with kidney failure, he died after having uncontrollable internal bleeding. It was April 20, 2011. It was quite a shock for him to go downhill so rapidly, because he had been doing well on the kidney dialysis. Things had appeared to have stabilized for him.

But I was selfish for not having thought about God and for never having picked up my Bible during those years when I was caring for Kenneth and managing everything else at the same time. I thought God had abandoned me then, but really I had abandoned Him.

After Kenneth died, I once again regained my relationship with God. My faith that had been so dear to me in Cambodia was restored. Everything in my life opened up for me. During those last years of Kenneth's life, I was drained, unhappy, and unable to talk with anyone about all that I had been working so hard to manage. After his death, everything changed. Once again my relationship with God and my faith were restored.

"Train up a child in the way he should go:
and when he is old, he will not
depart from it."
Proverbs 22:6
(KJV)

## Chapter 8
# Tia and Ty As Young Adults

During all the years I took care of Kenneth, I also continued to work, take care of our children Tia and Ty, be there for Kenny, and take care of our home. I never really felt as though I spent as much time with Tia and Ty while they were growing up as I wanted to. I wanted to be able to do more with them, play with them, talk with them, and be more involved in their lives. The demands created by taking care of Kenneth prevented me from doing that.

Both of our children grew up happy and successful. They have been and are still pursuing their dreams.

Tia graduated from the Yadkin Early College in May 2012. She earned her high-school diploma and her two-year degree from there.

Two years later, Ty graduated from Star Mount High School in May 2014.

Tia went on to study at Western Carolina University and graduated from there in May 2015 with a bachelor's degree in Communication Sciences and Disorders and a minor in Speech Pathology. She wants to continue her education by pursuing a degree in Sign Language.

In July 2015, Tia started as the Administrative Assistant at First Baptist Church of Sylva in the mountains in Sylva, North Carolina. She has grown up in and worked and served in Baptist churches since she was very little. During high school, she was an intern at Mountain View Baptist, her home church. In July 2018, Tia will have been at First Baptist Church of Sylva for three years. She loves her job.

Ty went on to study at the University of North Carolina in Charlotte. He graduated on May 12, 2018, with a bachelor's degree in Geology and a minor in Earth Science.

Both Tia and Ty are pursuing the dream of an education in America that my father wanted for me from the time I was very young in Cambodia.

Tia and Ty

Tia and Ty

"Then I heard the voice of the Lord, saying,
'Whom shall I send?
And who will go for us?'
And I said, 'Here am I. Send me!' "
Isaiah 6:8
(NIV)

## Chapter 9

# *Haiti Mission Trip*

I went on a mission trip to Haiti in February 2017 along with a group from my church. We called our team "Water Delight," and it consisted of Matthew Brown, David Cave, Paulette Ashley, and me. The first day of our trip we spent travelling. Our first flight was leaving from Charlotte International Airport, and we arrived at the airport with plenty of time to check our luggage. We got our tickets, and things were going smoothly until we got to the security checkpoint. Matthew was detained there due to a suspected bomb in his luggage. We were all surprised by this and stunned as the airport-security personnel kept asking him questions. I thought that this surely was the devil's work again, attempting to keep us from going on this trip to serve the Lord. We were all worried that our trip would end before it even started. Matthew was our group leader, so without him we would have been lost as to what to do. I prayed to God to please let him get through security. Finally they did let him through but only after a thorough search of his luggage, which led to the realization that he was, in fact, not carrying any type of explosive device or weapon.

We flew from Charlotte to Fort Lauderdale, Florida, and waited in the terminal there for a connecting flight to take us to Haiti. All of us decided to go in search of foods to eat because we knew it would be the last opportunity we would have to eat on American soil. We didn't have much time, so Matthew and Paulette decided to go get some chicken. David and I went to find some sandwiches. Then Dave and I sat down to eat our food and began to talk about our trip and what it would entail for all of us. We talked about how much we had sacrificed to go on the mission trip. We were all leaving our families to go to an impoverished foreign country with almost no drinking water. We had raised funds and spent our own money to fund the trip, and we were all taking time off from our jobs. Dave and I realized we would each need $10 cash for the immigration fee from the airport to our destination in Haiti. He didn't have any cash on him, and I said that I might have a 20-dollar bill and could get change from someone. Though we didn't realize it, the entire time we were talking about the trip, all that we had done, and the cash we needed, a woman sitting nearby was listening in on our entire conversation. Suddenly she turned around to us, handed each of us $10, and said, "Thank you for all of your service. No, I didn't realize how much you all have to put in. But I'm sure the Lord knows and I do now."

Dave and I were stunned. We couldn't believe that a total stranger overheard us and was willing to pitch in and help. At first I resisted the money but she insisted that we take it, and we thanked her. I thought about Romans 1:16 and said, "For I am not ashamed of the gospel, because it is the power of God that brings salvation to everyone who believes: first to the Jew, then to the Gentile." (NIV)

We rejoined our party and boarded the plane. Once we arrived in Haiti, the scenery was beautiful and the people welcomed us humbly and with great respect. We had come there to drill for water and help them find suitable drinking water and they knew all about this. They were grateful to have us there to help them.

I had an interpreter named Cole Carroll who helped me speak to the native people. I gathered a group from the local village and started talking to them about God. I told stories from the Bible as little children and adults stood around and listened carefully. A friend of mine, Nancy Gilbert, gave me gospel picture cards that she had created and laminated to use as aids in communicating with natives. The cards displayed the story of Adam and Eve and the story of Jesus Christ. Nancy travelled with me to Asia on previous mission trips and we used her picture cards then. Her cards were a crowd pleaser, and they made telling the stories more fun. I'm thankful for her donation and for the time she spent creating the picture cards.

While I got prepared with my cards, I asked if anyone in the group had been saved. No one knew what I was talking about. I asked if they believed in Jesus. Most of the people shrugged and a few shook their heads. A couple of them didn't even know whom Jesus was. Then I told them about heaven and hell and about how Jesus died on the cross for our sins. They weren't convinced. I asked if anyone wanted to go to hell forever, and the interpreter explained to me that their culture didn't have a word for hell, so he substituted the word *fire*. They all looked scared and the children said they didn't want to burn forever. Our mission team saved a whole group of people that day.

During our time in Haiti, we drilled for water and found three good wells that supplied water to around 10,000 people. The local villagers used a small pump and recyclables, bins, jugs, and canisters to collect the water to take back home to their families. Many people were carrying very large buckets and bags on the tops of their heads. There was one man to whom we'd witnessed during our mission who was thankful for our help. He had been working all day in the field and was travelling with his donkey and harvest through the area where the three wells were. To thank us for the water, he gave us a long stick of sugarcane, which we didn't want to take from him. However he insisted and we felt it would be disrespectful not to accept his generous offer.

That's me with the ponytail. I'm telling this Bible story to the standing crowd in the background. "Since they could not get him to Jesus because of the crowd, they made an opening in the roof above Jesus by digging through it and then lowered the mat the man was lying on. When Jesus saw their faith, he said to the paralyzed man, 'Son, your sins are forgiven.' "
—Mark 2:4–5 (NIV)

Paulette Ashley is telling the very same story at the same time to the young men seated in the forefront.

I'm sitting next to a Haitian woman who just got saved.

I'm pumping water from the new pump for the first time. It was very difficult to force the air out and pump the water at first.

"But to do good and to communicate
forget not: for with such sacrifices
God is well pleased."
Hebrews 13:16
(KJV)

## Chapter 10

# Ongoing Speeches and Special Thanks

In recent years, I have given a lot of speeches about my life at schools, churches, conferences, and communities. I've presented autobiographical speeches since the early 1980s. However while I was taking care of Kenny's dad, I didn't have time to give speeches. After his death in 2011, I began speaking again in earnest.

I was invited to give a speech at a church in Sparta through Matt Sheets's mother. I travelled there with a good friend, Darby Fife. I wasn't very familiar with the area and neither was she, so we left early. When we arrived in the town, we decided to stop for a bite to eat before going to the church. We found a little local diner and went inside. We found seats at the bar, and a woman dressed in casual-looking clothing with a cap turned around backwards on her head approached us. She had a pretty face, but she carried herself in a nonchalant manner. When she opened her mouth to take our order, we were startled by her lack of teeth. Her front teeth were gone and the rest of her teeth were starting to rot. She greeted us with a deep southern accent, and we gave her our order. We both ordered a sausage-and-egg biscuit.

We could see through a small window into the kitchen. The woman who took our order was chewing tobacco as she cooked.

Her assistant was a man who was smoking a cigarette. I could just imagine the ashes falling off the cigarette and into the food, and we both wondered exactly where she was spitting her tobacco. As she was preparing another table's food, we watched her drop an egg she had just scrambled on the floor. She exclaimed, "Five-second rule!" Then she scooped the egg up off the floor and put it back on the plate. Our mouths must have dropped open. We were shocked that she did that. The male server came out and served the floor egg to the other customer, and the diner started eating it as though it were nothing. We proceeded to ask for our food to go, paid for our order, and took the biscuits out with us. We didn't eat them. We just couldn't believe what we had seen.

This was one of countless adventures I've had as I've travelled and told others my story and shared how my experiences helped me grow to know Christ.

David Faidley, a correctional officer at the Sam Perdue Juvenile Center in Princeton, West Virginia, invited me to give a speech about my life and coming to know Christ through my experiences to the young incarcerated men at his facility. Deanne Fife had passed one of my business cards to him, and he had ordered some copies of my book for the center. He thought it would be a good idea to have me come and share my testimony with these young men. Darby Fife went along with me and introduced the discussion by singing an inspiring song.

Bodyguards stayed very near us for security while we gave our presentation. I did the invocation and then started by saying that we are all sinners and we all have skeletons in our closets. But I went on to say that anyone can change, and the time to do so is now. I told them that everyone has done something bad, but not everyone has gotten caught doing it. I wanted these young men to know that I was on their side in finding Christ.

By the end of my speech, I could feel the presence of God in the room. I knew that my story had reached the hearts of those young men because 19 of them raised their hands to be saved that day. I asked Officer Faidley if he would like to say the "sinner's prayer." He told me he had never done anything like that before and was a bit nervous, I think. But he did very well and was short, sweet, and to the point. After he finished, he said, "Siv, thank you very much." I was greatly applauded and thanked by many who were there. I felt elated and amazed that my testimony had made such an impact and assured people to believe in Christ.

There was one young man at the juvenile center who had already read my book. Officer Faidley told me he wanted to meet me. I was slightly apprehensive due to the many precautions we had already taken to ensure our safety while we were at the prison, but the young man approached me afterward and was incredibly kind to me. He expressed how much he loved my book and that he wanted to make sure he got a chance to meet me when I came to speak. He looked at me seriously and elaborated, "You have really turned my life around. I'm going to do good from now on. I'm going to turn everything around when I get out of here." I felt wonderful to know that my book and my speech had inspired him to change. I promised the young man that I will continue to pray for him, and I wished him well for his future.

*I would love to take this time and opportunity to say thank you to the many churches, schools, conferences, and communities for allowing me to spread the gospel through my story. I am grateful to have had the opportunity to have changed lives and to have brought people closer to God. I appreciate everyone who has taken the time to invite me to speak, to make the arrangements for my speaking engagements, and to attend and listen to my speeches.*

*Most of all,
I thank God for everything.*

CPSIA information can be obtained
at www.ICGtesting.com
Printed in the USA
LVHW07s0520200918
590752LV00016B/63/P